SCOTTISH CLUDGIE

(The good, the bad and the boggin')

Deedee Cuddihy

First Published 2021
Copyright©2021 by Deedee Cuddihy

ISBN 978 0 9930986 7 3

Published by Deedee Cuddihy
10 Otago Street,
Glasgow G12 8JH
Scotland

Cover design and technical assistance: The Lodger (Glasgow) Ltd.

Printed in Glasgow

Dedication

Everyone who contributed to this book deserves my thanks, especially Angela & Maureen; Ruth & her colleagues at the Mitchell Library in Glasgow; Jude; Maggie Ramage; Maggie C.; Clair; and C.M. who, despite his help, may still be the subject of his own little book, provisionally titled: "My really annoying Scottish husband".

Foreword

As a journalist, I normally have no hesitation about asking casual acquaintances and total strangers for their thoughts on any given subject. The focus of this book, however - "The Scottish Cludgie" - meant I couldn't be quite so gung ho in my approach. (Even I drew the line at enquiring of someone waiting alongside me at a bus stop if they had any interesting toilet experiences they would be willing to share.) Happily, I was still able to gather together more than enough excellent, cludgie-related material for this modest publication, covering everything from toilet paper to the difficulties experienced by lady golfers, in the 21st century, when looking for a place to pee.

**"Then oot cam her mammy,
She's goin' tae the cludgie,
Oh oh, ah buggered off
sharpish"**

(from "Cod Liver Oil and The Orange Juice",
the song by Ron Clark and Carl McDougall
made famous by Hamish Imlach)

I was one of seven kids and we were brought up in a room and kitchen in Kirkland Street in Maryhill, Glasgow. We shared a toilet on the ground floor with three other families. It had a high level flush, squares of newspaper on a nail for toilet paper and it was kept spotless. You didn't spend a lot of time in there, reading for instance, as there were other people wanting to use it. You took a candle with you at night and if it blew out, you couldn't see the toilet paper! But you also had a chamber pot in the house. Every family had a key to the toilet but you could also use a knife to flick the lock open if you needed to.

(Jim Divers, retired plumber)

We had our own bathroom but my auntie lived in a tenement with a shared toilet on the stair. It was kept immaculate but what I remember most about it was the big, solid wooden toilet seat - and my auntie cutting up squares of newspaper to use as toilet paper. She'd get a nail and hammer a hole through the corner of a stack of squares and then loop them on a piece of string.

(Maureen)

When it was your turn to do the stairs in a tenement, you'd also clean the toilet - no matter how clean it was already. And when you were using the cludgie, you'd never look up when you were sitting in there because there'd always be spiders.

(Ann)

I had a friend at primary school in Lanarkshire in the 1950s whose parents were Eastern European immigrants and they lived for a very short time in two rooms of a partially burnt out mansion with no toilet facilities apart from a bucket in a cupboard.

(Alan)

When I was pregnant my auntie got us a room and kitchen in Firhill, overlooking the canal. There was a shared toilet on the ground floor and when you went into the "cludge" you brought your own toilet paper - just a bit of newspaper - and there wasn't a key for it and you had a pail to use in the house if you didn't want to go there in the night.

(Ina, 85)

Residents of the Scottish border town of Galashiels are, understandably, not keen on their nickname of 'pailmerks'. It is said they got this name from days gone by when there were no toilets in Galashiels as we know them today - so inhabitants sat on pails. And if they sat too long, their rear ends would be 'marked' by the rim of the pail. The story does not explain what inhabitants of other towns in those days did to avoid this!

(from the internet)

My mum would say in the morning: *"Who's going to timpt the chanty?"* - take the chamber pot out to the toilet to empty it. It was accepted, in our house, anyway, that you were only supposed to pee in the potty and if there was a jobby in it, the cry would go up: "Who did the jobby in the chanty?" And we'd all say: "I didn't do that so I'm no' empyting it!". It was a proper china potty, with flowers printed on it.

(Maureen N.)

Annie Gibbons could rightly claim to be Govan's most popular housewife - for she's had no less than 300 visitors to her home this week. They've been visiting Annie's room-and-kitchen flat at 10 Luath Street to see her new bathroom which was converted from a bed recess.

For the past 17 years, the Gibbons family have lived with no hot water or inside toilet. When Glasgow Corporation announced in their redevelopment plan that houses in the area would not be demolished for at least another 15 years, Annie decided something had to be done.

She sought the help of (Raymond Young and other) architecture students from Strathclyde University who had been working in Govan and together they worked out a plan to fit a bath, w.c. and sink with hot water into the bed recess.

After visiting Annie's flat, one of her neighbours said: "I think it's wonderful - the best thing since sliced bread - and I can't wait to get mine done."

(from a report in The Govan Press in 1971, reproduced in 2013 in the book "Annie's Loo" by Raymond Young)

******

The flat I was brought up in had quite a small bathroom and I'm sure I remember there was a kind of fold-up wash hand basin that was designed to hang over the bath when you pulled it down from the wall.

(Rosie)

I'd never experienced a shared toilet until I went to art school in Glasgow in the 1960s and rented a room and kitchen in a tenement in Murano Street, in Maryhill. It was quite primitive. There was only a sink to wash in so I used to have a shower at the art school.

(Jim W.)

******

My family used to live in a tenement in Roystonhill, Glasgow which had a shared toilet on the landing. Then the year after they moved to a house with its own bathroom, I was born and my sister who is seven years older than I am, said I waited until then because I'm a snob!

(Britt)

There were no sinks in the shared toilets in tenements - people didn't wash their hands in those days . . . kidding! We washed at the kitchen sink and there were the public baths for actual baths with different days and times for males and females.

(Geraldine)

We lived in Paisley and had our own inside toilet but not a bathroom. There were public baths but we washed every day at the sink. We had a towel each and the routine was that you used a smaller part of the towel for the soap and water and the larger part for drying yourself. You wouldn't spend a long time in the toilet - because it was freezing in the winter and this was in the days before things like heated towel rails. My mum would wash our pants and socks at night and then she'd heat them up in the oven the next morning, to get rid of any dampness before we put them on.

(Isobel)

We had a proper bathroom in our house but until they moved to a new council house in the late 1950s, my aunt and uncle and my cousins lived in a flat in a three-storey building with no inside toilets. There was a beaten earth back court and sheds with dry toilets and an arrangement of a large bucket with ashes in it from the coal fires that would be sprinkled into the toilet with a wee shovel.

(Richard)

******

A crucial advance in plumbing was the S-trap, invented by the Scottish mechanic Alexander Cummings in 1775, and still in use today.

(from wikipedia)

The first time we ever experienced a dry toilet was on holiday in Stevenston, Ayrshire, where we rented a wee chalet - a hut, really - that had a dry toilet in a shed which would be emptied by a man who came around with a horse and cart and one of the local kids would shout out for everyone to hear: *"The shitie man's here!"* but it was usually pronounced *"shi-ee"* and could be abbriviated to: *"The shi-ee's here!"*

(Angela)

******

In the Second World War, the Crown of Scotland was hidden from the enemy in Edinburgh Castle, buried in a medieval toilet.

(from the internet)

The first time I experienced a shared toilet was when we went to Port Seton for a summer holiday one year, in the 1980s, and the flat we rented had a toilet on the landing which was a bit weird if you're not used to it. And then at the other end of the scale, we used to visit our Posh Auntie - which is how we referred to her - after she moved down to England where she lived in a bungalow - not a tenement - that had TWO bathrooms, one of them an ensuite and one with a bidet, things we'd heard of but never actually seen with our own eyes.

(Elaine)

We have three bathrooms in our house now so there's no need - like there was when we only had one - to let other family members know that you're planning to use it and how long you're likely to be, in case someone else has to use it more urgently than you do. One of the bathrooms is our ensuite and it's the rule that only my wife and I are allowed to use it.

(Iain)

My partner's mum spends two hours having a bath every Sunday afternoon so when we visit her, she warns you to use the toilet before she goes in but sometimes you're just about bursting by the time she's finished.

(Ellen)

******

We spent as little time in the bathroom as possible when I was growing up because it was always cold, especially in the winter when there would be ice on the inside of the window in the morning. That was in the days before heated towel rails which were a godsend.

(Isobel A.)

I was brought up on the family farm in Ayrshire and to avoid all of us children and our pals and the farm workers tracking dirt through the house during the day to use the toilet, my mother had one built outside, next to the coal shed. This was back in the 1940s and I can't remember what sort of toilet paper there was but a paraffin lamp had to be left burning in it at night during the winter to stop the pipes freezing.

(Morag)

By the time I was born, my grandparents were living in Troon in a house with two rooms and a row of sheds outside where the toilets were. I think each household had their own toilet and the area was white washed and very well kept. They were proper flush toilets with wooden seats which were very comfortable! I can remember, in the 1950s, watching my grandfather cut up copies of the Daily Record on the table, using a wooden rule to divide each page into four. Then, with a big darning needle, he'd thread each square onto a length of string which would be hung up on the inside of the toilet door, so you could easily reach out and take a piece off.

(Grace, journalist, who later worked for the Daily Record.)

We had soft toilet paper, Andrex, at home as far back as I can remember - I was born in 1949 - but my granny lived in a tenement in the Gorbals in Glasgow and shared a toilet on the stair with two other families and there used to be squares of newspaper on a nail.

(Boyd McNicol)

******

I think newspaper was better than the stuff that was like tracing paper because newspaper usually softened up a bit but Izal didn't.

(Chas)

In the 1950s, my parents emigrated from Scotland to Canada where I was born. We moved back when I was 11 and stayed for some time with my granny near Dumfries which was fine apart from her toilet paper which wasn't like the soft stuff I was used to but was the awful hard kind, like tracing paper. That was a real shock.

(John)

******

What a great invention soft toilet paper was! And so much better than the shiny, hard stuff in so many ways. You could use it to take off your make-up and you nail varnish AND blot your lipstick!

(Maggie R.)

When I became head of housekeeping at a big psychiatric hospital in Glasgow in the early 1970s, I discovered there was a hierarchy of toilet paper in operation. There was the Izel in boxes for the patients, rolls of Bronco for ordinary workers and soft toilet paper for office staff.

This seemed unfair to me so I asked a patient who worked in the stock room - and who these days would probably be considered to have had OCD tendencies - to count the number of sheets in all three types.

I was then able to calculate that, bearing in mind how much more of the cheaper papers had to be used to get a satisfactory result, the soft stuff was actually a more economical buy.

And so it was that we all got to use soft toilet paper - something that I still consider one of my greatest, professional achievements!

(Maggie C.)

In 1956, the manufacturers of Izal asked psychologists to do some consumer research into whether British people were ready for soft, unmedicated toilet tissue. More than 400 interviews later, the psychologists reported back: the market was "softening up" but faster in some places than others. In Glasgow, for instance, the psychologists found that many people still used newspaper.

(from the Wellcome Institute archive)

We had soft toilet paper at home but I learned to love the Izal toilet paper at primary school because of the noise it made when you pulled a sheet out of the box, so much so that I'd pull out more than I needed just to hear the sound. Of course, you couldn't put it back in the box again so I'd stick it in my knickers until I got back to the classroom where I'd hide it in my desk and use it to draw on.

(Madge)

I'm in my 80s but I can still remember, growing up, we used to get a box of oranges every Christmas and when they were finished, we'd use the squares of tissue paper that each orange had been wrapped in as toilet paper. It was orange, with blue printing on it, and quite soft.

(Morven)

******

I can remember visiting friends at their cottage in Ettrick in the Borders, years ago, and although they had a proper bathroom, they had a pile of that tissue that tangerines came wrapped in, to use as toilet paper. It was very soft.

(Viv)

When I was a student, one of the guys I shared a flat with used to get sandwiches from Subway and use the wrappers for toilet paper. They didn't always flush away and you'd see them floating around in the pan.

(Tom)

******

Myth: *"Toilet paper decomposes quickly, so I can just leave it under a rock." In fact, toilet paper can take anywhere from one to three years to decompose.*

(from the internet)

I once rented a room out to a guy who was a bit of an alcoholic. He'd been staying in the flat for a couple of weeks when I noticed that the toilet paper was being used up really quickly. Then I walked into the bathroom one evening and caught him eating it. I said "What the hell are you doing?" and he said "I can't afford food and drink so before I go to the pub, I eat some toilet paper to line my stomach." He claimed it was something they used to do in the French Resistance when their food supplies were running low. I said: "If you want to eat bog roll, you can buy your own."

(Dougie)

Dylan came home from nursery when he was about 3 1/2 and said he had a joke. I wasn't expecting much, so was preparing to fake laugh. Dylan: *"Why did the toilet roll roll down the hill? To get to the bottom!"*

(Julie on facebook)

******

We always put the toilet paper on the holder with the paper hanging outside because the other way, it picks up damp from the wall. Or that's what my gran insisted and we've always stuck with that in our family.

(Isobel)

Overheard two women having a chat on the bus from Dundee. One of them was telling a story about an elderly friend who'd become obsessed with checking the sell-by dates when doing her shopping. "I came across her in the supermarket last week, having an animated conversation with one of the sales assistants. I said: "What's going on, Jessie?" And she said: "I'm just telling this young man that I can't find the sell-by date on this." and I said: "What is it you're buying?" and she held up a pack of toilet rolls."

(Deedee Cuddihy in the Herald Diary)

At primary school in New Stevenston, Lanarkshire in the 1950s, I had my arm broken one day when I was knocked to the ground by one of the bigger boys in the rush for the toilets at the morning interval. The boys' toilets were dreadful. The section with the urinals was open to the sky and there were competitions to see who could pee over the wall and onto the pavement on the other side. The cubicles were to be avoided at all costs. There were wooden seats screwed directly onto the porcelain pans and, on the one occasion that I can remember feeling the need to use them, I ran home instead because I lived nearby.

(Charlie)

I was involved in a session where P7 pupils meet with pupils from the high school they'll be going to and get to ask them questions about what it will be like, and one of the main things they wanted to know was: "Is it true that you get your head flushed down the toilet on the first day?" as if that was some kind of normal, initiation ritual.

(Rowan)

I was at primary school on the south side of Glasgow in the 1950s and early '60s, in the days when there were separate playgrounds for boys and girls and there was a toilet block in each one, with both buildings almost open to the skies at the top. If you needed to use the toilet, you were supposed to go at the interval but the problem was, there was a terrible bully called Jeannie McCludgie* who often used to stand guard at the entrance to the toilet, ready to grab you by the hair, drag you inside, push your head down the pan and pull the chain flush. But you wouldn't dare tell the teacher why you hadn't gone at the interval, for fear that Jeannie McCludgie would do something even worse to get back at you.

(Maureen S.)

*Name changed to protect the contributor!

When I was at primary school, the older girls would try to drag the younger boys into the girls' toilets just to embarrass them.

(Alastair)

******

When I was at high school in the 1960s, the cubicles in the boys' toilets were always full of pupils smoking and there'd be a permanent cloud of cigarette fug hanging above the partition walls.

(Andrew)

The girls' toilets at the secondary school I went to in Jordanhill were always full of boys smoking. The toilets were in the playground and it was always a male teacher who was on playground patrol and he wouldn't come into the girls' toilets so that's why the boys smoked in ours.

(Lucy)

At my high school, most of the tough girls hung around in the toilets at break time, smoking and chatting with the cleaners. The smell of cigarettes was so strong that your clothes would be reeking and I was worried that my parents would think I'd started smoking.

(Katie)

I developed a phobia about cleaning cloths after seeing one draped over the metal pipes under a sink in our primary school toilets. This was almost 50 years ago and I can still remember coming out of the cubicle, looking towards the sink and seeing, underneath it, what appeared to be a rat, and almost jumping out of my skin with fright. My phobia is so bad that I never allow any cloth or rag that we use in our house for cleaning to be hung up to dry. Once it's used, it's sealed in a plastic bag and thrown in the bin immediately.

(Caroline)

Oh dear, what can the matter be?
I'm feart tae go tae the lavat'ry.
I've no been since two weeks last
Saturday.
I know who's hidin' in there!

(Billy Connolly)

******

". . . and a listener has got in touch to say the girls' toilet in her school was allegedly haunted by a ghost called Malky."

(Ashley Storrie on the Ashley Storrie Show, BBC Radio Scotland)

"Parents' fury as Scottish primary school changes to unisex toilets."

Angry parents have told how children went back to their Midlothian primary school after half-term to find the toilets had been made unisex. Mothers said daughters were now embarrassed to use the facilities while boys have been spotted urinating in the sinks. A spokeswoman for Midlothian Council said the change was temporary while the school was being refurbished.

(from a news report in the Scotsman)

The girls' toilet in our secondary school had an adjustable blower on the hand dryer so there was always a queue of us, waiting to use it to dry the sweat patches from the armpits on our white shirts.

(Sally)

I went to a private school for girls in Glasgow where the toilets were absolutely shocking, particularly the wooden toilet seats which were cracked in places and if you shifted about on them in the wrong way, your bottom would get nipped and you'd end up with a blood blister which was extremely painful.

(Clair)

I remember being traumatised during my first week at primary school in Tillicoultry when I went to the toilet, locked the door and couldn't get out again. It made me wary of locking the door in a public toilet ever since. I'd rather lean my bag up against the door and shout *"Someone's in!"* if someone tries to get in.

(Yvonne)

I can remember in my first week at primary school, asking the teacher if I could go to the "bathroom" - because that's what we said in our house - and she said: "Do you need a bath?" And when a child put their hand up and said: "I need" she would say: "What do you need?" Basically, she was just trying to get us to use the word "toilet" so there would be no question of what it was we actually wanted to do.

(Marie)

I got a job in a biscuit factory when I left school - I was so young I was still wearing ankle socks! - and the woman in charge of the recipe room I worked in was called Vera Love who was so proper and lady-like that if you needed to go to the toilet, you weren't allowed to use the word "toilet" and you certainly didn't say bog or cludgie or khazi; you had to call it "the bathroom".

(from "I Love Tunnock's Tea Cakes and lots of other biscuits")

I worked as a teacher for a few years and we had a terrible head master who was obsessed with the amount of toilet paper the staff were using. At meetings he'd regularly remind us about the need to use only what was absolutely necessary, and glare at us in an accusing way!

(Linda)

I was a secondary school music teacher and, at the first job I had, I would occasionally have to nip out to the toilet after taking registration, leaving my class alone for a few minutes, at which point the head of department would take great pleasure in standing right outside the toilet door and shouting through to me: *"Are you in there, Miss?"* which was obviously very embarrassing.

(Laura)

You might have heard the strange claim that if someone knocks on your door in Scotland and needs to use the toilet, you are bound by law to let them enter. However, this has been debunked by the Law Commission, which says it "cannot find evidence that it was on the statute book". The law experts say the myth may have grown around local custom and point to Scottish people's "strong sense of hospitality".

(from the internet)

We get several groups of people who work outdoors and come in on a regular basis to use our customer toilets, like traffic wardens and delivery drivers.

(Mitchell Library staff, Glasgow)

I sometimes pretend to be pregnant when I need a pee and there are no public toilets in the area. I'll nip into the nearest pub or cafe, put my hand on my waist at the back, stick my stomach out and say *"I'm really sorry - I'm pregnant. Could I please use your toilet?"* It works every time. I feel bad when they're very sympathetic but it's a sure fire way to use a customer toilet without actually being a customer!

(Jude)

A block of public toilets in the historic town of St. Andrews has sold at auction for almost £200,000 - about four times the guide price. The stone toilet block was snapped up by a mystery developer from the west of Scotland who plans to convert it into a house. The listed stone building which still boasts its male and female toilets, attracted about 15 potential buyers and had a guide price of £50,000.

(from a news report, 2007)

I suffer from Shy Bladder Syndrome which makes it almost impossible for me to use a public toilet or any toilet that isn't in my own house. Family and friends are amazed at how long I can go without peeing.

(Fiona)

******

I find it really difficult to have a "number two" anywhere except in my own house; maybe at a good friend's house, if I was really desperate. Neither of my sons would have a "number two" at their secondary school because the toilets were so disgusting. We lived a mile away and they'd run home at the interval if necessary.

(Brenda)

I was taking my two kids up to Oban on the train for a day out and my daughter who was 4 at the time, said she needed to go to the bog.

After she'd finished having a pee, I looked around for the flush mechanism and saw that there were two handles on the wall, both with their labels torn off. Well, one was red, the other brown and it seemed obvious to me that the brown one was the flush, so I pulled it.

Within seconds, the train had screeched to a halt, causing my daughter to fall to the ground and bang her head. We made our way back to our seats, my daughter crying, me cursing whatever had caused us to stop so abruptly.

As the train started up again, the following announcement came over the tannoy: *"May I remind passengers using the toilet that the flush mechanism has a red handle and the emergency stop mechanism has a brown handle. Thank you."* In my defence, can I just point out that this would not happen if the handles were properly labelled!

(Anna)

I've got a horror of those toilets on the trains with the automatic sliding doors. When I get inside one I have to say to myself three times: "Lock the door, lock the door, lock the door."

(Joyce)

I used to do the occasional DJ set at a club in Glasgow where the only toilet was in a cupboard right beside the floor space where the bands played and if you didn't lock the door after going in, it would sometimes swing open during a performance, exposing the occupant to the full glare of the other clubbers. Every time I used it, I had to remind myself: **"Lock the door! Lock the door!"**

(Jasmine)

"Comfort & Joy" painting by the late
Tam Smith, with the kind permission
of his daughter, Sylvia Smith

Original toilet with wooden seat in the
Tenement House, Glasgow

This urinal is dedicated to three men who participated in the Scottish Highland Clearances.

These men took part in what is now recognised as a form of Central Government endorsed ethnic cleansing.

Through their greed and bigotry, they and others have been instrumental in destroying a centuries old Scottish Highland way of life.

PLEASE FEEL FREE TO PAY THEM THE RESPECT THEY ARE DUE

COLONEL FELL

In more recent times this man continued the Highland Clearances process on the island of Lismore through enforced evictions of the indigenous population.

Higland Clearances protest urinal, the Lismore pub, Partick, Glasgow

Donald Trump toilet paper in a Leith
flat, Edinburgh

Cafe in a former public toilet, Gibson St., Glasgow

Toilet attendant, Gibson St., Glasgow,
1977

Classic graffiti, Glasgow

Graffiti, ladies' toilet, Mitchell Library,
Glasgow

**When you spend
a penny, you're
saving water.**
This toilet has ~~two~~ HOT flushes ! !!
by using the smaller — 0.0s
button you'll be helping us
save water.

This sign has been made

Hot flush graffiti in M&S ladies'
toilet, Glasgow

"Lassies lavvies" toilet sign, shopping
centre

Barbara Davidson ceramic mural,
ladies' toilet, Queen St. station,
Glasgow circa 1970

View from portable eco bog, Eilean
na Gamhna, with thanks to T.
Dawson, V. Gunn and E. Kennedy

I can remember going to the GFT (Glasgow Film Theatre) for the first time with my mum when I was about 12 and being very impressed with the perfume dispensing machine that was fixed to the wall in the ladies' toilet. You put in six pence, I think, and would be sprayed with a choice of one of four or five different fragrances. Very sophisticated! Ladies' toilets also had little plastic bags for used sanitary products, that had an outline of a crinoline lady printed on them in black. And I used to love going to weddings in posh hotels because the ladies' "powder rooms" were so glamorous.

(Janine)

In the ladies' toilets of all the clubs I went to in Glasgow, there would be an older woman there with a selection of all the things you might need when you're on a night out, like deodorant, a hair dryer, sanitary products, chewing gum, Chupa Chups, even make-up, in case you'd been crying! There'd be a box for a donation or a tip for what you used and I think maybe the women - who were usually from abroad - didn't get paid for being there but would have to make a profit from the stuff they provided.

(Sarah M.)

"But, as a wheelchair user, my all-time scariest experience involving a pub toilet happened a few years ago in Glasgow. I opened the door of the accessible loo to discover a couple having sex on the floor. Rather than feeling embarrassed and getting out of my way, they instead shouted unintelligible abuse, locked me out and carried on where they'd left off. Since I really needed to pee, I went and got the bouncer to forcibly evict them."

(from the internet blog "Ouch! A wheelchair user's survival guide to pub toilets" by Laurence Clark, 2010)

I quit my job in a night club when the manager asked me to clean the cocaine off the toilet seat lids because they were expecting a visit from the police. I said: "I'm not paid to do that."

(Rosie S.)

******

Allegations that a nightclub in Glasgow has secretly fitted a two-way mirror to allow male guests to spy on the women's toilets "as a bit of fun" are being investigated by police and council licensing officers.

(from a news report, 2013)

I saw a member of the Scottish band, Arab Strap in the toilets of a club and I asked him if he was who I thought he was, and he said: *"Yes, but I'd rather not say too much while my d**k is in my hand."* I said fair enough and left.

(from the internet)

******

Men's toilets are awful - you always have to make sure when you're using urinals that you just look straight ahead and don't even glance at the guy peeing next to you, in case he thinks you're checking out his penis.

(David and Craig)

I remember my first gay male friend telling me that they called the men's public toilet in St. Vincent Place off George Square in Glasgow *"The Palace of Lights"*, although I don't know why.

(Dorothy)

******

If you don't want to get caught out when you're cottaging in a public toilet, the two of you go into a cubicle together but one of you stands in a plastic carrier bag so no one coming in will see two pairs of shoes under the door. It will just look like one man with a bag of shopping.

(Michael)

Visitors to the popular Botanic Gardens in the West End of Glasgow were relieved when they heard that the public toilets there, which had closed during the lockdown, were going to re-open. But relief turned to anger last week when it was discovered that only the ladies' toilet was re-opening - as a unisex facility. Said one of the attendants:

"The new arrangement has not gone done well, particularly with women who say they don't like sharing toilet facilities with men. And I can't say I blame them. I've seen men come in and not close the stall doors, not flush, and then not wash their hands which I obviously have to pull them up on."

(from a news story, August 2020)

I'll use the men's toilet if there's a queue and I'm desperate because they always have two or three cubicles in them. I did that once in a pub and the guys who were there cheered when I came in! But I didn't let that put me off.

(Susan)

My daughter is only a few months old and I usually take her out in a baby carrier, strapped to my chest. Every once in a while I've been caught short when I've been out with her on my own and have had to nip into a public toilet for a pee. No one standing beside me at the urinals has ever made a comment about it. I suppose that's a story I'll be able to tell her when she grows up!

(from The Wee Guide to Scottish Men)

We went on a family holiday to a camp site in the Borders that had composting toilets and the kids spent hours shining a torch down them to see how they worked.

(Graham)

******

I have a friend who fell asleep in a composting toilet at a music festival and only woke up when it was being towed away on a trailer.

(Iain S.)

Scotland's most remote public toilet
just isn't up to the jobbie

It is said to be Britain's most remote
and expensive public toilet - built on
an uninhabited island which is home
to over 200,000 seabirds. But less
than four years after being installed
on Handa, three miles off the
northwest coast of Sutherland, it
seems the £50,000 comfort stop is not
completely flushed with success. The
composting eco toilet is failing to
keep up with demand as it tries to
cope with a boom in tourists. Said a
spokesperson for the Scottish Wildlife
Trust: "The toilet on Handa is
operational but could be composting
faster. It is struggling to keep up with
the demand and needs tweaking."

(from the Daily Record 2016)

In days gone by, most people in Scotland lived in the country and had no toilets of any sort so would just go outside. Many farms had a shared manure heap – for human and animal dung – which was dug into the fields as fertilizer. In towns, some houses might have a 'dry' toilet or privy, without any water for flushing. People used to keep their clothes in the same room as the privy because they thought that the smell would keep the moths away from their clothes.

(from the internet)

I can remember when I was around 9 or 10, in the late 1950s, exploring around the site in our small town where they were building a new church. On one area of waste ground - where there used to be a frog pond - there was a lean-to wooden hut, open at both ends, where the workers had dug a latrine to use as a toilet, with a narrow wooden plank suspended across the length of it to sit on.

(Martin)

Other very early toilets that used flowing water to remove the waste are found at Skara Brae in Orkney, Scotland, which was occupied from about 3100 BC until 2500 BC.

(from wikipedia)

We were brought up in Glasgow but my mum's family were from Benbecula in the Outer Hebrides and we used to spend the whole summer up there when I was at primary school. We loved it! It was just a but and ben so I don't know how we all fit in!

There was no toilet but there were two lochs just nearby. What was called the Front Loch was where they got the water for drinking and cooking and the Back Loch was for peeing in and washing which had a flat rock that you could walk onto. You would never mix the two up.

For a number two, you would go into the surrounding fields and squat down behind certain plants, depending on the season. There was no toilet paper so you used leaves but not grass. And not just any leaves. There were certain ones you could use and others you couldn't.

My granny boiled up water in a cauldron over a peat fire to wash the sheets and we'd help to wring them out and then bring them outside to dry over the heather, pinning each corner down with a rock.

(Christine)

I was brought up down in England and we were travellers. In those days, you didn't have toilets in your wagon or your caravan and there were only toilets and washing facilities for travellers much later on so we'd often just do our business out in the open, and use grass for toilet paper, or leaves if there was no grass. My mam had one of those galvanised tubs and she'd wash our clothes in it and then wash us! I've lived in Scotland for years now, in a house, but I'll still use the outdoors if I have to, and grass or leaves. But my son, he's 18, and there's no way he'd do that - never!

(Billy, street preacher and tree surgeon)

We went to a caravan site for holidays and then you used the toilet block because there weren't toilets in caravans in those days. That was a real trial for me, due to the number of Jenny-long-legs dancing around the light bulbs at night. That was another thing to be terrified of!

(Louise)

This was in the 1960s and my parents and my brother and I found ourselves living, temporarily, in a cottage in Dumfries and Galloway with no indoor plumbing. We got metal churns of fresh water from a nearby farm, washed in the burn and the only place to put our Elsan chemical toilet was in the entrance porch to the cottage where my brother was sitting one morning, having a crap, when the postman chapped the door, opened it without waiting for a reply, and handed Alistair our post, never batting an eyelid.

(Sheena)

As a lady golfer on the wrong side of 50, when someone suggests playing at a new club, this is the first thing you ask: *is there a toilet on the course?* Obviously there will be facilities in the club house itself but if you're playing 18 or even nine holes, you'll probably need an on-course pee at some point - especially if you're behind a group of really slow men - and if there aren't any portaloos dotted around the course, it's "au natural" which is a lot easier for men than women. Gullane has good portaloos on the 7th green; Troon also has nice ones; and St. Andrews has real toilets for women on their course.

There aren't any on-course toilets at the club I'm a member of but the ladies have an "al fresco" spot on the 6th green as well as a tree on the 10th green that you can duck down behind plus a ditch in the woods between the 15th and 16th greens. No need for paper hankies or anything - just a quick shake does it!

(Ruth)

I live in quite a rural area and I've got a neighbour, a woman of 80, who says she'll pee in a bush if necessary when she's out on a walk. She's got no problem with it.

(Sylvia)

A sheriff has warned the Trump Organisation that it has put its staff at risk of prosecution under anti-voyeurism legislation after its "frivolous" complaint to police about a woman urinating near its Aberdeenshire golf course. In a highly critical judgment, Sheriff Donald Corke said that the woman was entirely within her rights under Scotland's land access laws to be on the course and to relieve herself in a considerate manner. Her distress at being photographed while urinating by staff with their mobile phones without her knowledge, and then charged, was very real.

(from the Guardian, April 2017)

I've got female friends who are ramblers and hill walkers and they all have *"shewees"*, the device that women can use to pee standing up. I asked my sister for one for my birthday and it's great! Especially for me because I have two artificial knees and it's difficult for me to squat down. You do have to practice at home at first but it's fine once you get the hang of it. It was great during the lockdown when you'd be going to visit friends in their gardens and couldn't use their toilet because of restrictions but you would have had some lunch with a bottle of wine and cups of tea and then have maybe quite a long walk home - and all the public toilets were shut! So before I started on my walk home, I'd nip behind their garden shed or the bushes, wheech down my joggers and have a pee - standing up! Fair flushed with success I was!

(Maggie R.)

******

I've got three children, all boys, and I encourage them to pee in the garden. It's good for it! We live in Ayrshire with no near neighbours so no one can see them.

(Sarah)

* *"Introducing urine to one's garden space is actually an age-old practice that's used by gardeners and farmers around the world and, depending on what your garden needs, it can be used in a variety of ways."*

(from the internet)

"A delicate whiff of carbolic greeted a capacity audience at Dundee Rep on Saturday night as Chris Rattray's "The Mill Lavvies" returned to the theatre after a ten year absence. Set in the early 1960s, the play follows five male mill workers for whom the "lavvies" provide a respite from the noise and drudgery of their working day."

(Dundee University Review of the Arts, 2012)

When I was a student, my uncle got me a job in the summer holidays at a plumbers' merchant in the east end of Glasgow and the guys I worked with took any opportunity to use the toilets because they were situated beside the company office and meant they could have a good look at the girls who worked there when they went past.

(Sam)

******

I sell more toilet seats in January than any other time of the year. It's because of all the drinking that goes on at Hogmanay and toilet seats get wrecked.

(Jaz, hardware shop owner)

Asked about the infamous *"Worst Toilet in Scotland"* scene in his 1996 film **"Trainspotting"**, director Danny Boyle reveals that, in reality, the bathroom set was anything but grimy. ***"It was meticulously clean,"*** he says, adding that all the faecal-looking elements were, in fact, different kinds of chocolate.

(from the internet)

I run a vintage clothes shop in the West End of Glasgow and we get the occasional celeb coming in including, one afternoon a few years ago, the American actress **Frances McDormand** and her husband, **Joel Coen**, the director film maker who immediately approached me and said:

"Excuse me, do you have a rest room I could use?" I said "yes" but warned him that it was a very old-fashioned, Edwardian one with an overhead cistern and a chain flush, not to mention a few mushrooms growing on the wall because there was a bit of a dampness problem.

But he was fine with that. In fact, I didn't recognise them but my colleague did as soon as they came into the shop which explained why she had been winking at me the whole time they were there!

(Lesley)

I was using the toilets in a shopping centre one day and had put my bag down on the floor in front of me when a hand appeared under the cubicle door and grabbed it by the strap. A bit of a tug of war ensued but I managed to keep hold of it and by the time I got out, the person who had tried to steal it had disappeared.

(Clair)

Poo in the Loo at Glasgow Art Show

A ladies' toilet that was turned into a temporary exhibition space during a modern art festival in Glasgow had to be shut down - after a member of the public used the loo for the purpose it was orignally intended. Said a spokesperson for Glasgow International 2014: "The toilet at the McLellan Galleries in Sauchiehall Street had not been in operation for some years and was being used to screen a video. A member of the public apparently didn't notice that the water had been shut off and that the loo was being used as an art space. Maybe they were desperate - or perhaps it was a comment on the work. The toilet had to be shut temporarily for cleaning purposes."

(Deedee Cuddihy in the Herald Diary 2014)

Road works in Gairbraid Avenue, Maryhill - near the Burgh Halls complex - have uncovered the remains of an old, below ground gents public toilet, hidden under tarmac for decades. It prompted one 85-year-old Maryhill man to recall that another, above ground, gents toilet, further up the road but long since demolished, had been nicknamed *"The Maryhill Opera House"* due to the fact that it was frequented by customers from a nearby pub who, after chucking out time, were inclined to burst into song while using the facility.

(Deedee Cuddihy in the Herald Diary, 2012)

SHETLAND Library is launching a new round of "Bards in the Bog", the popular project displaying poetry in public toilets. Entry is open to everyone of any age, and people are invited to submit original, short poems to be installed on the back of toilet doors. The theme is entirely open, but the important rule is that poems must be short – a maximum of 16 lines to be displayed in large font on an A4 poster so they can be read comfortably by readers seated a few feet away.

(from the Shetland News online, 2020)

In high school I had a friend whose father was a gynaecologist and it was always interesting using their bathroom when I went to visit because there would be a selection of the latest medical journals to read on the toilet. I learned a lot about urinary tract infections and other conditions!

(Helen)

One of the guys I share a flat with has a subscription to *"The Economist"* that he keeps in the bathroom and that's what we all read when we're on the bog.

(Josh)

I read when I'm on the loo - most often a food magazine or a cook book. A chapter of **Elizabeth David** will usually do it.

(Anne)

I've got a friend who has a wonderful selection of books in his bathroom, in a proper bookcase.

(Linda S.)

We have a collection of "Funny Scottish Books" in our bathroom, next to the bog, contributed by the author.

(Maggie Cuddihy, the author's sister-in-law . . . !)

In our Govan tenement, *'the cludge'* was one of my favourite hideouts, a place of privacy when ever-present humans became too much of a burden. Each tenant on our landing had a key to it; ours hung just inside the door in the lobby. It was here I came to scrutinize the pages of the Sunday Post. Perched comfortably on the wooden toilet seat, I chuckled with glee at the antics of *"The Broons"* and *"Oor Wullie"*.

(from *"Blue Above the Chimney"* by Christine Marion Fraser)

I have a friend who gets the *"Broons"* and *"Oor Wullie"* annuals every year and keeps them in the toilet.

(Kate)

My father was terrible for reading in the toilet. He spent hours in there every day with the newspaper.

(Marianne)

I think people like to read in the bog because reading helps you relax and once you've relaxed, it's easier to have a number two. And it's a bit of peace and quiet.

(Diane)

Maybe it's just me but I find it easier to have a number two if I've done a crossword before I go into the bog.

(Sarah G,)

******

I used to work with a man who would say: "I'll be in the office" when he was going to use the toilet, and he'd take the crossword in with him.

(Sue)

Our mum was brought up in a tenement in Tollcross, Glasgow in the '20s and '30s with a shared lavie on the stair - the half landing - and she told us stories about Mr. Johnson who would, famously, always be in there doing the crossword and you'd knock on the door and he's say: *"I'll not be long - I've just got to get 12 across and 6 down."* And there was a woman on their stair who also did the crossword and Mr. Johnson would sometimes knock on the toilet door when she was in and say: *"Mrs. Laurie - did you get 29 down?"* or whatever clue he was having trouble with.

(Nuala)

My flat mates were supposed to look after my pet rat, Brownie when I went away for the weekend. However, they had a party and at some point, someone let Brownie out of her cage and when I got back, she was nowhere to be found. Then we became aware of a slapping noise coming from the toilet and discovered Brownie, trapped in the U bend. Fortunatley, we managed to fish her out and she survived!

(Tulip)

I was in the kitchen one evening when I heard a strange splashing sound from the bathroom next door. When I went to investigate, I saw that there was a large brown rat in our toilet, swimming around and attempting to get out by trying to grasp the slippery edge of the pan. Horror-struck, I flipped a bath mat over the edge of the toilet - to give the rat something to grip on to - and ran out of the room. Imagine my relief when, no longer hearing any splashing sounds, I returned to discover that the rat had, indeed, made its escape and had vanished outside, presumably through the hole in the bathroom skirting board from whence it had probably come.

When my husband returned from the pub and I told him what had happened, he said I shouldn't have helped the rat escape but should have, instead, flushed it down the bog.

(Amy)

******

Rats are excellent swimmers – they can hold their breath for three minutes and tread water for three days. If they want to get in your toilet, they will.

(from the Guardian, with thanks to Jude Stewart)

Back in the 1960s I went out occasionally with a guy who really liked football and he invited me to a match which turned out to be the Celtic v Dukla Prague one in Glasgow.

I'd never been to a football match before and at half-time I suddenly became aware of this river of what I thought was water streaming past our feet and I looked around to see where it was coming from - I thought maybe a pipe had burst somewhere.

Then I saw all these men facing the back wall of the stadium and realised they were all having a pee! It was literally like a waterfall coming down the steps of the stand we were in.

And I said: *"My God - look! Those guys are all pissing. That's absolutely disgusting!"* The bloke I was with looked really embarrassed that I had called attention to it and told me to keep my voice down.

(Lorna)

******

"Plans are being drafted just now to modernise the underneath of the new Enclosure opposite the Stand. We intend having a Powder Room for the ladies in this area."

(Celtic Football Club news, December 1966, with thanks to Jim)

We were late arriving for a footbal match at Ibrox and noticed that the bloke running one of the mobile burger vans had opened the side door of the van and, while still standing inside, was peeing up against it.

(Gordon)

******

I'm 61 but I've become quite adept at getting my mobile phone out of my pocket to take a call with one hand while I'm standing up having a pee. I'm a taxi driver and I wouldn't want to miss a fare.

(Bob)

A Glasgow music hall has survived for more than 150 years due to the fact that minimal toilet facilities meant rough and ready audiences simply peed where they were standing. While other wooden music halls of the Victorian era had a life span of approximately 25 years before burning down, the *Britannia Panopticon* in the Trongate was so saturated with pee that fires couldn't take hold and the amonia helped preserve the timbers. Music hall performers in those days were also in danger of being peed on, by rowdy audience members watching from the balcony.

(from a news report)

"A lovely gig at Glasgow Theatre Royal - and then back to my dressing room where a woman was taking a s***. In fairness to her, it was in the bathroom part of the dressing room, rather than on the floor or the table."

(stand-up comedian Adam Kay on Twitter, October 2021)

Going to the gents' toilet was the highlight of an evening - over 50 years ago - when I was presuaded to attend an amateur opera production in Castle Douglas town hall. A member of the cast was performing in a full suit of armour and, at the interval, I went to the bog and there he was, trying to have a pee with his armour still on! It was quite a sight.

(Willie)

And Deedee Cuddihy tells us that on a family outing to the Royal Highland Show earlier this week, her primary school age son reported, after a trip to the gents' toilets, that one of the farmers using the facilitiy was so drunk, he had been standing in the urinals and peeing out onto the floor.

(from the Herald Diary, June 1990)

A mechanic who was told by one of the directors of the company he worked for in Aberdeenshire that he and his colleagues should do what they did on his farm and "go round the back of the sheds if they were that desperate for the toilet" has been awarded £16,000 by an Employment Tribunal in Dundee.

(from a news report)

If my brother was in the bathroom and you went to the door to ask what was taking him so long, he'd say *"I'm brushing my teeth"* but in a really strained voice, as if he was actually mid-crap but was trying to disguise the fact. It became a family joke.

(Alec)

******

My two boys go into the toilet together at home - and they never close the door.

(Iain)

When we were growing up, my wee brother went everywhere with our dog, including to the toilet. You'd hear him in there, having a pee, and chatting to the dog at the same time.

(Eddie)

******

We were visiting our daughter and were amused to see our three-year-old grandson in the garden, attempting to fill his water pistol by peeing into it! We weren't sure if it was just for fun or because he couldn't be bothered going inside to the sink.

(Claire)

My wee niece was seven when my beloved cat, Islay, died and she knew I was really upset about it because I had called my sister when it happened and and burst into tears over the phone. When I visited them a few days later, my niece said to me: "Auntie Frances, will you come to the toilet with me?" and when we got in there, she said: "Now you can talk about Islay if you want to" I thought it was amazing that, even at that young age, she recogised that the toilet can be a place of refuge where confidences can be exchanged.

(Frances)

I can remember eating my lunch in a toilet cubicle for the first few days at a new college where I didn't know anyone. It was just soup and a roll. And it was quite a nice toilet.

(Sally)

******

At entertainment venues there's always a queue outside the ladies toilets and when you get in there, you'll sometimes see two and even three girls coming out of the same cubicle. I wouldn't do that but I suppose it can save time and also you can talk about what's been happening.

(Shan)

"Haven't seen anyone in years holding their child over a gutter at the side of the road to have a pee."

(Jennie)

******

I can remember watching the telly when I was a child and thinking it was strange that, although characters in soap operas and plays often announced that they were going to make a cup of tea or go upstairs to bed, or have a shower, none of them ever mentioned needing to go to the toilet.

(Sheena, actress)

No one else in the family is supposed to use our ensuite but I suspect if I went home right now, I'd find my son in there, playing a game on his phone.

(Sylvia)

******

When I was growing up in Dundee, you'd say *"keech"* instead of *"shit"* or *"shite"*. In fact, there was a kind of poem about keech which was: *"The people they're funny in Brechin. They never say shittin', they always say keechin'."*

(Sandra, in The Wee Guide to Scottish Swearing")

At the primary school I went to back in the late 1950s, we used to shout ***"Keech toley bum fart!"*** to each other in the playground.

(Pete Kirley in "The Wee Guide to Scottish Swearing")

******

In my family, we called number twos "broonies".

(Tommy)

"I had a shower, went to the toilet . . . just a number one!"

(Andy Murray revealing to the world what he did during a break at Wimbledon in June, 2021)

******

When I was a child, we called peeing a wee-wee and a dump was a two-two.

(Linda S.)

A dung beetle walks into a bar and asks *"Is this stool taken?"*

(Sarah Williams on facebook, sharing a joke told to her by daughter, Izzy)

About Deedee Cuddihy

Deedee Cuddihy is a journalist who was born and brought up in New York but has lived in Glasgow since the "Big Storm" of 1967 (which she slept through). Or was it 1968? After finishing art school in Glasgow, she realised being an artist would be too difficult - and being an art teacher would be even more difficult. So she became a journalist and has been one ever since. She is married to a Scotsman and has two grown up children - plus four granddaughters. "The Scottish Cludgie" is the 16th in her Funny Scottish Books series, the other titles including the best-selling "I Love Irn-Bru", "Only in Dundee" and "The Wee Guide to Scottish Women". She lives in a flat with only one bathroom.